21st Century Skills Library

I0894922

COOL SCIENCE CAREERS

METEOROLOGIST

MATT MULLINS

Published in the United States of America by
Cherry Lake Publishing, Ann Arbor, Michigan
www.cherrylakepublishing.com

Content Adviser
Edward J. Hopkins, PhD, American Meteorological Society

Credits
Photos: Cover, pages 1 and 10, ©Jeff Greenberg/Alamy; page 4, ©iStockphoto.com/patrickheagney; page 6, ©Peter Arnold, Inc./Alamy; page 9, ©Caitlin Mirra/Shutterstock, Inc.; pages 12, 17, 21, 23, and 28, ©Photolibrary; page 15, ©Nick Cobbing/Alamy; page 16, ©imac/Alamy; page 18, ©iStockphoto.com/bonniej; pages 22 and 24, ©David R. Frazier Photolibrary, Inc./Alamy; page 27, ©Ryan McGinnis/Alamy

Copyright ©2011 by Cherry Lake Publishing
All rights reserved. No part of this book may be reproduced or utilized in any form or by any means without written permission from the publisher.

Library of Congress Cataloging-in-Publication Data
Mullins, Matt.
Meteorologist/by Matt Mullins.
p. cm.—(Cool careers)
Includes bibliographical references and index.
ISBN-13: 978-1-61080-034-1 (lib. bdg.)
ISBN-10: 1-61080-034-6 (lib. bdg.)
1. Meteorology—Juvenile literature. 2. Meteorologists—Vocational guidance—Juvenile literature. I. Title.
QC863.5.M85 2011
551.5092—dc22 2010038926

Cherry Lake Publishing would like to acknowledge
the work of The Partnership for 21st Century Skills.
Please visit *www.21stcenturyskills.org* for more information.

Printed in the United States of America
Corporate Graphics Inc.
January 2011
CLSP08

METEOROLOGIST

TABLE OF CONTENTS

CHAPTER ONE

UNDERSTANDING WEATHER

Paul was 4 years old when he awoke to see branches littering the backyard. It was October 13, 1962. The previous

Meteorologists help warn people when bad weather is on the way.

day, a huge storm had passed over his home in western Washington State.

The winds had hit the trees high above the ground. Paul saw trees at the edge of his yard that were twisted 20 feet (6 meters) above their roots. Street signs were down. This had been the most powerful storm in Washington since 1880, according to some experts. They called it the Columbus Day Storm, and it wrecked areas of the Pacific Northwest. It was probably the strongest West Coast storm of the 20th century.

Gary was 5 years old when his father was caught in a snowstorm in the Chicago area. Gary's dad was in a car with friends from work when the huge storm hit. It was 2 days before his father was able to make it home.

Weather has fascinated Paul and Gary ever since those storms in their youth. Now they are meteorologists. They study the **atmosphere** and forecast, or predict, the weather coming to an area.

The atmosphere surrounds Earth in five layers. Some scientists believe the outermost layer of the atmosphere ends halfway to the moon, about 60,000 miles (96,561 km) from Earth! In the atmosphere, heat from the sun, gases in the air, tiny particles, and water vapor mix together in various ways. These combinations create wind, clouds, rain, snow, and storms such as hurricanes and tornadoes.

The atmosphere is complicated. Meteorologists study the atmosphere. Different kinds of meteorologists specialize in different kinds of work. *Research meteorologists* study the atmosphere and weather. They use **satellites**, radio, radar, and various other tools. Research meteorologists usually work as scientists at universities.

Forecast meteorologists work for government agencies or private companies. These scientists focus on predicting

A meteorologist gathers weather data from instruments on a tower that overlooks the Amazon rainforest.

weather. Their predictions sometimes go to the public, such as the work of the National Weather Service. Forecast meteorologists who work for companies do things like predict how the wind will carry pollution from a factory.

Forensic meteorologists study what the weather conditions were like at a specific time in the past. They are often asked to present this information in legal cases. For example, a driver may explain that he hit a person on the road because glare from the sun temporarily blinded him. A forensic meteorologist will study weather data for that time and place, and will let the police know if the driver's story is likely to be true.

Broadcast meteorologists work for radio or television stations. They share their predictions of weather with the public on Web sites, radio, and television news broadcasts. Most on-air weather people are meteorologists, trained in atmospheric science. Some, however, are not. They are reporters whose job is to share information, including information about the weather.

Most meteorologists enjoy their work because every day is different. No one storm is like another. The weather can't be easily predicted. How many times have you heard a forecast and made plans, but then you were disappointed when the weather turned out differently? It doesn't happen most of the time—meteorologists are very good at what they do. But sometimes the weather fools even these smart, well-trained scientists!

LEARNING & INNOVATION SKILLS

Have you ever thought about how important weather is? Sometimes we think of it only in terms of whether we can play outside or not. We forget that weather shapes history.

Weather can cause droughts, which are times when little or no rain falls. The Mayan civilization disappeared during the 700s and 800s. Scientists believe a long drought forced Mayans to leave their homeland. The Akkadians were one of the world's early civilizations. They vanished sometime around 2100 BCE because of a long period of drought. A storm kept the Mongols from successfully invading Japan in 1274 CE. Bad weather helped the Allied army surprise German forces on D-Day in June 1944. That changed the course of World War II (1939–1945).

Can you think of recent weather events that have caused major problems?

Storms can cause major damage to homes, businesses, and other property.

CHAPTER TWO

A DAY ON THE JOB

When Steve arrives at work each morning, he first hears a report from the meteorologists who have worked all night. Steve works for the National Weather

Meteorologists work together to come up with the best possible weather predictions.

Service (NWS) at a location near Milwaukee, Wisconsin. The NWS is part of the U.S. government's National Oceanographic and Atmospheric Administration (NOAA).

Steve is a forecast meteorologist. He has been predicting weather for 25 years. At the morning **briefing**, he learns what the main weather event of the day is expected to be. It may be a winter storm. It may be severe weather, such as a lightning storm or a tornado. Then Steve studies **data**. He looks at current conditions such as temperature, **humidity**, and wind speed. He reviews images from satellites that circle Earth.

Steve uses computers to study weather patterns. He creates maps and drawings for the Internet and for television weather reporters. Steve forecasts the weather for the coming 7 days and sends these forecasts to newspapers, radio stations, and television stations. When it looks like a serious storm is coming, Steve announces it to the public on NOAA Weather Radio and the NWS Web site. The National Weather Service warns us when we should be careful driving or working or playing outside.

Gary is a broadcast meteorologist. He works at a television station in Madison, Wisconsin. He delivers weather reports on the evening news. Gary's day at work begins with checking instruments at the station. He makes sure all of the equipment is working properly. Then he looks at weather maps, at weather data from Steve's office, and at satellite and radar information. He reviews the forecasts his coworkers have made earlier that day.

Then Gary begins typing forecasts. He prepares a forecast for the next 7 days and a forecast for the next 10 days. Gary prepares different forecasts for different Wisconsin cities—Madison, Janesville, Platteville, and Lancaster. These forecasts usually differ from one another in certain ways. Maybe the

Some people get their weather information from TV broadcasts.

temperatures will be different in Platteville and Lancaster. Maybe Janesville will get more rain than Madison.

Next Gary records forecasts for radio stations. He e-mails audio files of the forecasts to stations to use on the air. Then he begins to work on the evening news forecasts. Gary creates graphics to use on television. He puts information on the TV station's website. He sends out forecasts on Twitter and posts them on Facebook.

Then Gary does his 5 o'clock news broadcast. After that, he does the 6 o'clock news. Gary usually goes home for dinner. Then he returns to the station. He prepares images for the 9 and 10 o'clock broadcasts. He also plans the work schedule for all the station's weather reporters and forecasters for the next week. Gary gathers more weather information for his next day of work.

Gary is up early the next day to work on radio programs. Then he takes a nap before heading back to the TV studio after lunch. He often visits schools to talk to classes about his work. Gary has a busy, but exciting, job.

Paul is a research meteorologist at a university in Fort Collins, Colorado. He begins his day by checking the computers at the radar meteorology laboratory. He also answers coworkers' questions about their computers.

Paul and his coworkers study the atmosphere. They discover new things about weather. A few years ago, his lab made important discoveries about lightning in severe storms.

Paul's group proved that a 20-year-old theory about lightning was correct. Lightning forms when winds quickly lift clouds. Rising air cools as it lifts and rubs against ice crystals. This rubbing causes lightning.

21ST CENTURY CONTENT

Meteorologists study the atmosphere and weather. **Climatologists** also work in atmospheric sciences. They look at weather, too. But they study the **climate** by looking at weather patterns over long periods of time—decades, centuries, and even longer!

One way climatologists learn about weather from thousands of years ago is by studying ice cores. Scientists drill ice samples from deep within glaciers. They study the trapped air inside the ice. Tree rings, samples from the ocean floor, and samples of earth also offer clues to weather patterns of the past.

In recent times, climatologists have become concerned about dramatic changes in Earth's climate. They predict that big climate changes will occur in the next several decades. What do you know about climate change or global warming?

Ice core samples can provide information about past weather events.

When Paul is not helping colleagues with computer problems, he works on radar data. He helps sort and study the ways ice and water droplets in clouds behave. The work of research meteorologists helps forecast and broadcast meteorologists better understand how weather develops. Research meteorologists help other meteorologists produce more accurate forecasts.

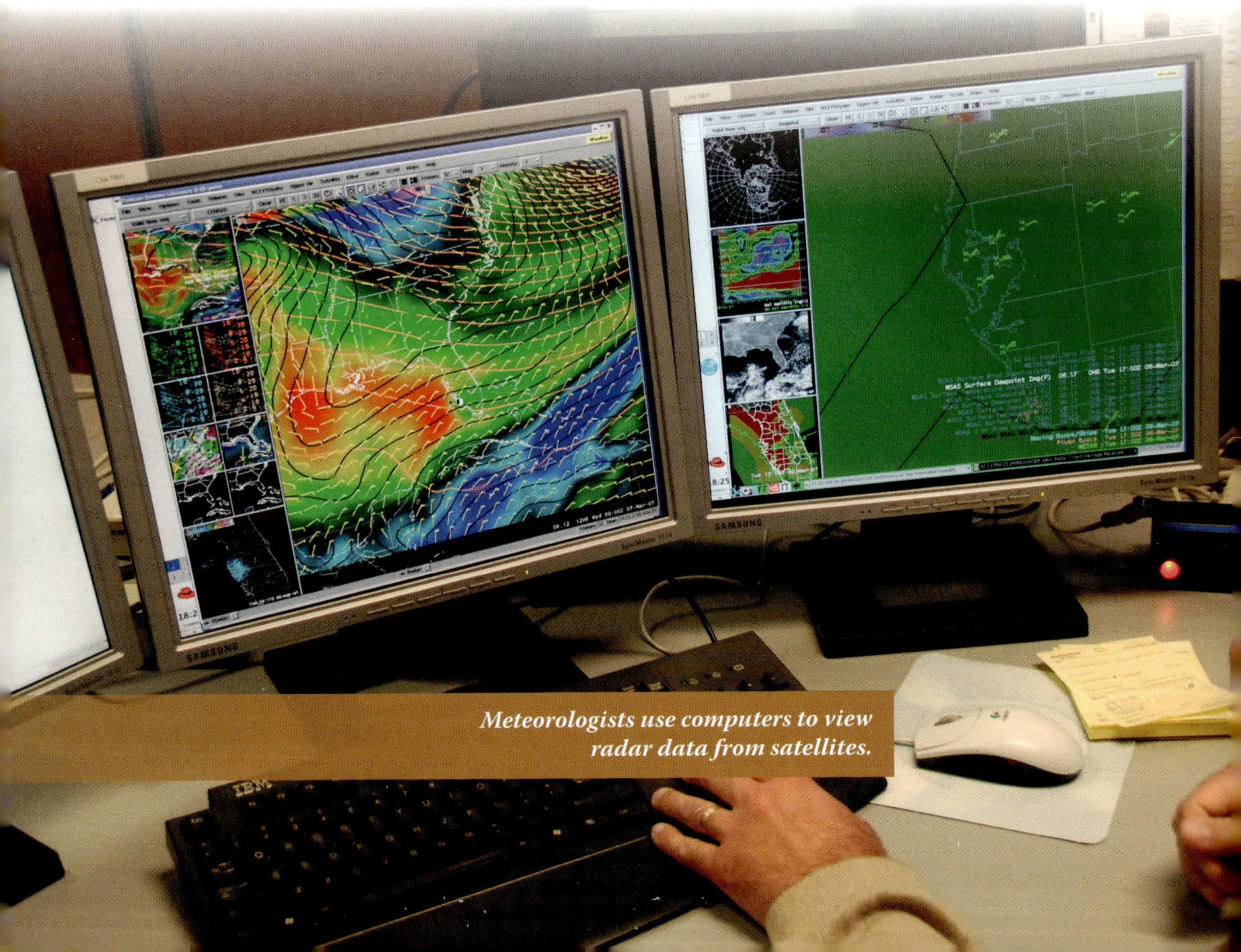

Meteorologists use computers to view radar data from satellites.

Radar data can show weather patterns for a large geographic area.

CHAPTER THREE

BECOMING A METEOROLOGIST

If you want to become a meteorologist someday, you can start preparing now. Study mathematics. Become good at it.

Math skills are important for meteorologists.

Meteorologists rely on math for calculating the ways in which air, water, wind, and other elements work together. If you enjoy working with computers, keep at it. Meteorologists do much of their work with computers.

Try measuring the weather. Get a thermometer and put it outside. Use a bucket to collect rain and measure how much falls. Observe clouds. Watch storms as they happen. Just be sure to watch from a safe place! Do you think it is interesting to record how much rain falls and what the temperature is from day to day? You may already be a junior meteorologist!

You will have to go to college to become a working meteorologist. Most broadcast meteorologists have bachelor's degrees in atmospheric sciences. Some have degrees in communications or journalism. Some have both science and communications degrees! Most broadcast meteorologists have studied at least a little of each.

Forecast and research meteorologists usually have taken more courses in atmospheric science than broadcast meteorologists. Some have also taken courses in earth science fields such as **hydrology** and **oceanography**. They may study advanced math and computer sciences. That's because meteorologists gather data, analyze it, and produce reports. They work to increase the knowledge we have about the atmosphere and weather.

LEARNING & INNOVATION SKILLS

Meteorologists use many scientific instruments in their work. Thermometers are used to measure temperature. **Barometers** are used to measure the pressure created by air in the atmosphere. Wind gauges help determine how strong the wind is, and rain gauges measure **precipitation**. Some meteorologists use radar to scan the atmosphere for small particles and ice crystals.

What kinds of new tools do you think meteorologists may use in the future? Which of the existing tools do you think they will continue to use?

Most forecast and research meteorologists have more than a bachelor's degree. These scientists usually have master's degrees or doctorates, which require staying in school longer.

One more thing helps if you want to become a meteorologist. Steve, Gary, and Paul all love helping people. Each of them contributes to better, more accurate weather forecasting.

Wind gauges help meteorologists learn more about storms.

They help us prepare for the day ahead. They warn us when bad weather is coming, and tell us when it is best to stay inside and when we can safely go outside. Meteorologists do important work. By helping us anticipate weather, they help us stay safe!

Sometimes students have a chance to talk to a meteorologist about his job.

Some meteorologists work outdoors.

CHAPTER FOUR

METEOROLOGISTS IN THE FUTURE

Meteorology is sure to change in the next several decades. Satellites, radar, and computers continue to

Meteorologist use many tools to keep an eye on weather patterns.

get more accurate, more powerful, and faster. Improvements in these tools will help meteorologists. Satellites have **sensors** that collect data. The data is used to make images. Many satellites also carry radars. These tools gather a lot of information from the areas they scan.

Soon satellites will take temperature readings throughout the atmosphere. We'll know the temperature at one spot as well as the temperature 100 feet (30.5 m) above that spot. If the temperature is different, it may have an impact on what future weather will develop.

As satellites and radar gather more data, and as computers process that data faster, meteorologists will be able to make predictions in 15-minute time periods. They may be able to tell you what the weather will be tomorrow at 12:30 p.m. and then at 12:45 p.m.! Some National Weather Service forecasts attempt this already but not a full day in advance. Such predictions, though, will continue to grow more and more common over longer periods of time.

Another way in which meteorology will change is in how we get our forecasts. Many people watch the local evening news less and less these days. Instead, they get weather information from Twitter, Facebook, and National Weather Service Web sites. They may watch video forecasts on their computers or use weather **apps** on mobile phones. Broadcast meteorologists need to keep up with new ways to provide weather information.

LIFE & CAREER SKILLS

As the climate changes due to global warming, the future of meteorology changes with it. Global warming affects the climate everywhere on Earth. Weather patterns are changing, and some places will get colder while others will get warmer. Some places may get more severe storms. Some places that get a lot of rain now might face droughts. Some climatologists even predict that Europe may enter a new ice age in as little as 50 years!

It won't just be meteorologists who are affected by climate change. People in nearly every profession will have to deal with the changes. Think of an adult you know. How might that person's job change due to shifts in global climate? How do you think changes in weather and climate might change the work you want to do when you grow up?

In other ways, though, meteorology may not change much. Although they may be able to predict weather changes every 15 minutes, few meteorologists think weather can be predicted more than 10 days in advance. Meteorologists seem a lot more confident telling us what the weather will do today than telling us what it will do tomorrow. Ask a meteorologist what the weather will be next week, and you may see

Mobile equipment helps meteorologists go wherever they need to study the weather.

that person squirm a little. Weather will always be complicated. Climate change might even make it more complicated. We may never see highly accurate forecasts past 14 days in the future. That's because most weather systems tend to gradually break down after several days.

One thing we can be sure of, though. Meteorologists will continue to learn more about the weather and the atmosphere. They will continue to use new and old tools to do their work. Meteorologists will always strive to learn more and to keep us informed about the weather.

Do you have what it takes to become a meteorologist?

SOME WELL-KNOWN METEOROLOGISTS

Howard Bluestein (1948–) teaches meteorology at Oklahoma University. In 1977, he began organizing students to help him learn more about tornadoes. He invented several ways to study them, including Doppler Radar.

Margaret LeMone (1946–) served as president of the American Meteorological Society (AMS) in 2010. She is a senior scientist at the National Center for Atmospheric Research in Colorado. She was the first chairperson of the AMS Board on Women and Minorities.

Lewis Fry Richardson (1881–1953) was a mathematician who introduced the use of math in weather forecasting. Weather forecasting became more precise because of its use of math and high-speed computers that can perform complicated mathematical computations.

Verner Suomi (1915–1995) invented the spin scan radiometer, an instrument used by weather satellites. He founded, with Robert Parent, the Space Science and Engineering Center at the University of Wisconsin–Madison. The center helped develop one of the first and most successful satellites that provided weather satellite imagery to meteorologists and television broadcasters. It was launched in December 1966.

Warren Washington (1936–) has been a senior scientist at the National Center for Atmospheric Research in Colorado since 1975. He was one of the pioneers in computer modeling of Earth's climate. He also served as chairman of the National Science Board from 2002 through 2006. He has written almost 200 articles on meteorology and climatology.

GLOSSARY

apps (APS) tools used to find information or perform a task that can be downloaded to a mobile phone or other device

atmosphere (AT-muh-sfeer) the layers of air and gases that surround Earth

barometers (buh-ROM-uh-tuhrz) instruments that measure the pressure exerted by the atmosphere

briefing (BREE-feeng) sharing of information or instructions

climate (KLY-muht) the average weather over a period of years

climatologists (kly-muh-TAH-luh-jistss) people who study climates

data (DAY-tuh) facts and information

humidity (hyu-MIH-duh-tee) the amount of water vapor in the atmosphere

hydrology (hye-DRAH-luh-jee) the study of water on or below Earth's surface and in its atmosphere

oceanography (oh-shuh-NAH-gruh-fee) the study of oceans

precipitation (prih-sih-puh-TAY-shuhn) the amount of liquid water or ice deposited on the ground by weather

satellites (SA-tuh-litess) a manufactured object designed to orbit Earth, the moon, or another body in space

sensors (SEN-surs) instruments that can detect changes in heat, sound, pressure, or other characteristics and send the information to a computer or other device

FOR MORE INFORMATION

BOOKS

Gaffney, Timothy R. *Storm Scientist: Careers Chasing Severe Weather*. Berkeley Heights, NJ: Enslow Publishers, 2009.

Housel, Debra J. *Weather Scientists*. Minneapolis: Compass Point Books, 2009.

Kjelle, Marylou Morano. *A Project Guide to Wind, Weather, and the Atmosphere*. Hockessin, DE: Mitchell Lane Publishers, 2010.

WEB SITES

FEMA for Kids
www.fema.gov/kids
Find out how to stay safe during weather emergencies and other kinds of disasters.

Sky Diary—Kidstorm
www.skydiary.com/kids
Learn more about tornadoes, hurricanes, lightning, and storm chasing.

Weather Wiz Kids
www.weatherwizkids.com
Discover links to games, pictures, and information about the weather.

INDEX

ABOUT THE AUTHOR

Matt Mullins has a master's degree in the history of science from the University of Wisconsin–Madison. He writes about science and technology, business, engineering, food and wine, and other topics as a writer and journalist. He has written 13 children's books and has begun writing and directing films. Matt lives in Madison, Wisconsin, with his son.